1.4

You have read lots of stories this year. Which story is your favorite so far?

This book is full of characters that are going places. A frightened bear gets lost in the city, and a pesky pig gets into all kinds of trouble. You will also read about a class trip to the forest and other stories about nature.

Read on! See what Treasures you will find.

HOUGHTON MIFFLIN
Reading
Treasures

Senior Authors
J. David Cooper
John J. Pikulski

Authors
Patricia A. Ackerman
Kathryn H. Au
David J. Chard
Gilbert G. Garcia
Claude N. Goldenberg
Marjorie Y. Lipson
Susan E. Page
Shane Templeton
Sheila W. Valencia
MaryEllen Vogt

Consultants
Linda H. Butler
Linnea C. Ehri
Carla B. Ford

HOUGHTON MIFFLIN
Reading
A Legacy of Literacy

HOUGHTON MIFFLIN   BOSTON • MORRIS PLAINS, NJ

California   •   Colorado   •   Georgia   •   Illinois   •   New Jersey   •   Texas

Cover and page photography by Tony Scarpetta.

Cover illustration by David McPhail.

Acknowledgments begin on page 227.

Printed in the U.S.A.

ISBN: 0-618-25780-2

9 10 DW 11 10 09 08 07 06 05 04

We Can Work It Out   12

Pet Show
by Mary Gold
illustrated by Pedro Martin

"Let's go see the Oak Tree
Road's Pet Show," said Joan.

Chan's Gift
by Mack Duffy
illustrated by Tungwai Chau

Chan needed a gift.
"Mom likes to cook," he said.
"I can get Mom a cookbook."

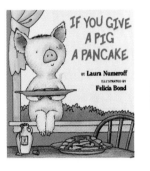

fantasy

✓ Taking Tests

Phonics Library:
Clues from Boots
Lou's Tooth
A Clean Room

Clues from Boots
by Tina Mendosa
illustrated by Bill Brandon

"Thank you for keeping
Boots while I go on this trip,"
said Drew. "His clues will let
you know just what to do."

Additional Resources

Big Book

No, No, Titus!
written by Claire Masurel
illustrated by
Shari Halpern

On My Way  Practice Readers

Joan and Coach Snow
by Sonia Ramos

Nell's First Day Kit
by Kate McGovern

What Can You Do?
by Ryan Fadus

Theme Paperbacks

The Puddle
written and illustrated
by David McPhail
🎗 **Bank Street College Best
Children's Books of the Year**

Busy Bea
written and illustrated
by Nancy Poydar

Internet

Visit www.eduplace.com/kids **Education Place®**

Read at school **Accelerated Reader®**

Read at home www.bookadventure.org **Book Adventure**

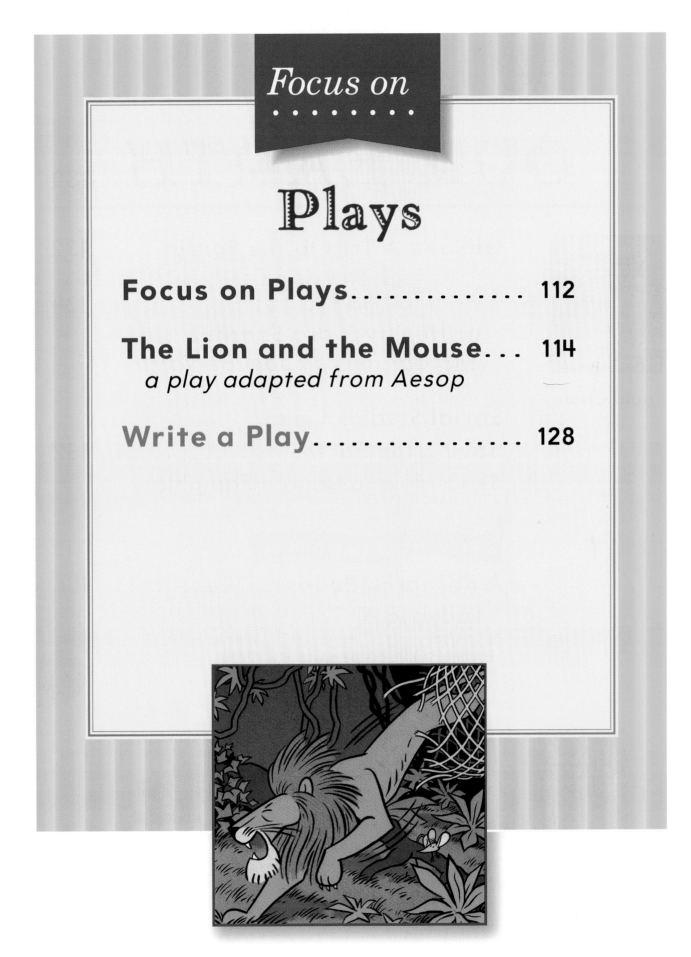

Plays

OUR EARTH 130

A Fine Spring Day
by Gregory Kang
illustrated by Brian Lies

"Frog," asked Cat, "what's up on this fine spring day?" "I am jumping in mud!" croaked Frog.

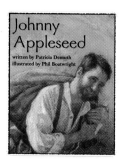

Choosing the Best Answer. **214**

Glossary. **216**

Phonics Library:
Hen's Big Show
Writing Home
Sam Sundown's Problem

10

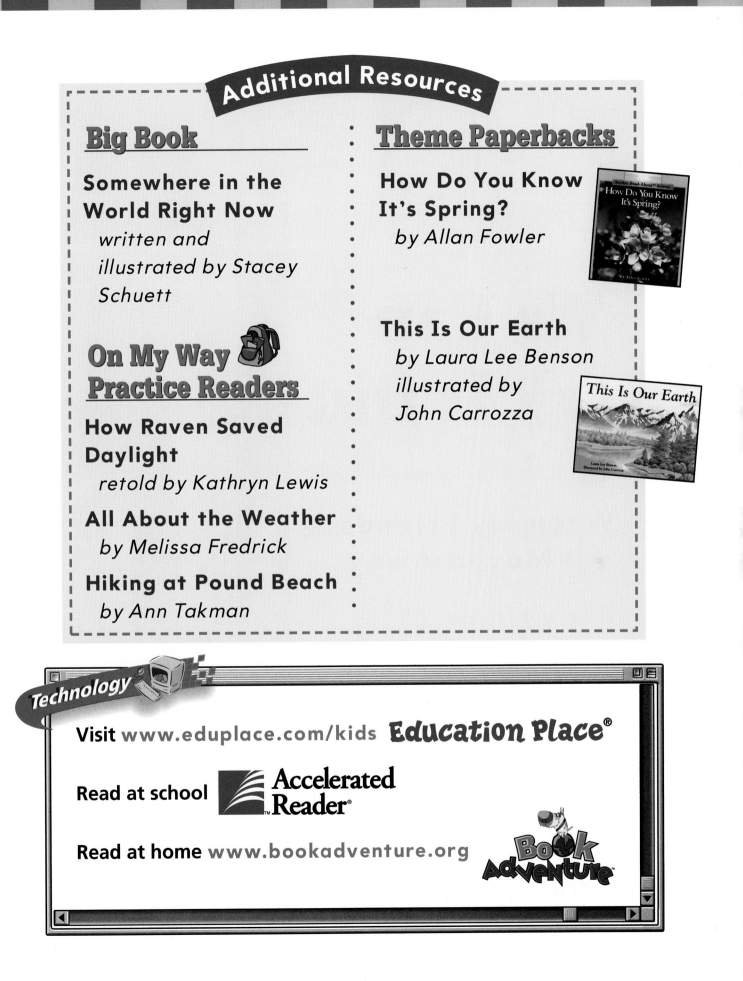

Additional Resources

Big Book

Somewhere in the World Right Now
written and illustrated by Stacey Schuett

On My Way Practice Readers

How Raven Saved Daylight
retold by Kathryn Lewis

All About the Weather
by Melissa Fredrick

Hiking at Pound Beach
by Ann Takman

Theme Paperbacks

How Do You Know It's Spring?
by Allan Fowler

This Is Our Earth
by Laura Lee Benson illustrated by John Carrozza

Technology

Visit www.eduplace.com/kids **Education Place**®

Read at school Accelerated Reader®

Read at home www.bookadventure.org Book Adventure

We Can Work It Out

Read Together

When My Friends All Moved Away

When my friends all
   moved away
I thought I wouldn't last
   a day.

Now I visit them by bus
And wonder why I made
   a fuss.

by Steven Kroll

That Toad
is Mine!

by Barbara Shook Hazen • pictures by Jane Manning

Our Pet Toad

The next story you will read is about two boys who share everything — until they find a toad!

Words to Know

again	hard
both	toad
gone	road
or	hoptoad
want	know
turn	

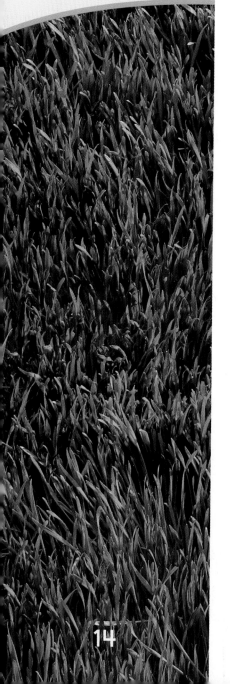

Practice Sentences

1. We both want to take our pet toad home.
2. Do you know if it's your turn or my turn?
3. It's hard to keep track.
4. You can take it home again.
5. Oh no! The hoptoad is gone!
6. It went down the road.

Meet the Author and the Illustrator

Barbara Shook Hazen has always wanted to be an author. Some of her favorite things are swimming, traveling, and eating pizza.

Jane Manning lives in Connecticut with her dog, Pumpkin. She likes to draw children learning new things.

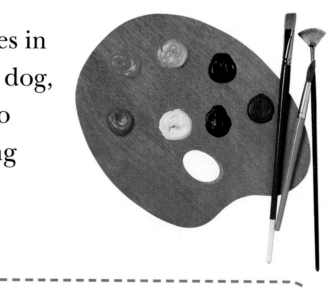

Internet

To find out more about Barbara Shook Hazen and Jane Manning, visit Education Place.

www.eduplace.com/kids

That Toad is Mine!

by Barbara Shook Hazen • pictures by Jane Manning

Read Together   As you read about the two boys in this story, stop and think about the things they do together.

John and I like to share
our toys, our food, and what we wear.

We share a book.
We share a bike.
We share a game that we both like.

19

We share a drink of lemonade.
We sit and sip it in the shade.

A sip for me, a sip for John.
We sip until our drink is gone.

21

We share our crayons and our cars.
We share a bag of candy bars.

When one is left, what do we do?
To share, we cut the one in two.

23

Then one day beside the road,
what do we see?
A big fat toad!

I look at John, John looks at me.
How can we share the toad we see?

We can't share a toad the same
as books or candy or a game.

"I want that toad."
John says, "Me too.
But we can't cut one toad in two."

"I know!" I say.
"Here's what we'll do.
A day with me.
A day with you."

"No way," says John.
"I don't agree.
A hoptoad needs one place to be."

I'm mad at John.
He's mad at me.
The two of us do not agree.

While we're mad, the little toad
keeps on hopping down the road.

"Your fault!" John says.
"No way!" I say.
"It's all your fault it hopped away."

I am so mad, I kick a stone.
I say to John,
"I'm going home!"

33

John looks at me.
He runs up quick.
He gives that stone a good hard kick.

"My turn," I say.
I run up quick.
I give that stone a harder kick.

A kick for me.
A kick for John.
We kick until our mad is gone.

We kick until we're home, and then,
John and I are friends again.

Think About the Story

1. How can you tell that the boys are friends?

2. What do you think the boys will do the next time they find something they both want?

3. How would you solve the problem in the story?

Create an Online Review

Tell others how you felt about *That Toad is Mine!* Create a review on Education Place.

www.eduplace.com/kids

Problem Solving

Could the boys' problem be solved in another way? Act out a solution with a partner. Take turns speaking, and listen carefully.

Creating

Write a Sign

Make a Lost Pet sign. Describe the pet and draw a picture of it. Hang up your sign.

Tips

- Write a list or sentences.
- Use good describing words.

Skill: How to Read a Poem

- **Read** the poem aloud.

- **Listen** for rhyming words.

- **Think** about how the poem makes you feel.

Hug O' War

I will not play at tug o' war.

I'd rather play at hug o' war,

Where everyone hugs

Instead of tugs,

Where everyone giggles

And rolls on the rug,

Where everyone kisses,

And everyone grins,

And everyone cuddles,

And everyone wins.

by Shel Silverstein

Sharing

I'll share your toys, I'll share your money,

I'll share your toast, I'll share your honey,

I'll share your milk and your cookies too —
The hard part's sharing mine with you.

by Shel Silverstein

A Story

In a story, the writer makes up what happens. Use this student's writing as a model when you write a story of your own.

A good **title** sometimes tells who the main character is.

A good **beginning** sets the scene.

Ricardo Decides

Ricardo had a problem. Jack wanted Ricardo to go to his house on Sunday. Ricardo told Jack, "I want to go to your house on Sunday, but I made a deal with my family that I would go with them to look for new baseball cards."

Jack said, "Think about what to do, and then let me know."

Ricardo didn't know what to do. So he spoke to his mom and dad. They said, "Go to Jack's house first. At two in the afternoon, we'll go get the baseball cards."

Ricardo called Jack and told him the new plan. The problem was solved.

Dialogue makes the character come alive.

The **middle** tells what happened.

The **ending** brings the story to a close.

Meet the Author

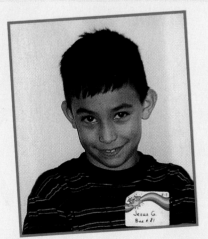

Jesús G.

Grade: one

State: Michigan

Hobbies: baseball, soccer, collecting cards

What he wants to be when he grows up: a baseball player

A Bear Book

In the next story, read to find out what happens to a bear who gets lost in the city.

Words to Know

afraid	look
any	good
bear	books
follow	someone
most	anything
tall	inside
water	outside
idea	

Practice Sentences

1. We can't go outside to play.
2. Is there anything to do inside?
3. Someone says, "Let's read books."
4. That's a good idea.
5. I look in a book on bears, and here's what I learn.
6. Some bears fish in the water.
7. Don't follow any bear you see.
8. Most bears are afraid of people.
9. If a bear stands up tall, don't get close!

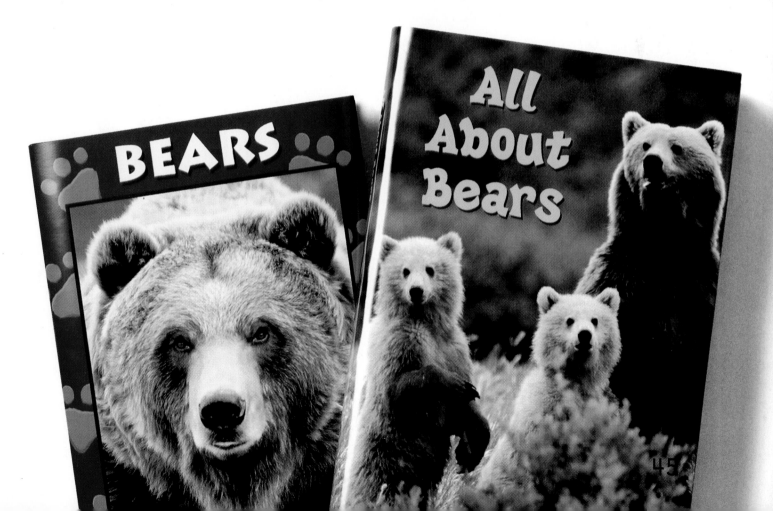

Meet the Author and Illustrator

David McPhail studied art at school. His advice for children who want to become artists is, "Draw, draw, draw!" He says, "Share what you are good at with others."

Internet

You can visit Education Place to learn more about David McPhail.
www.eduplace.com/kids

46

Lost!

David McPhail

 Read Together   Make sure you understand what is happening in the story as you read.

I am walking down the street when I hear
someone crying.

It's a bear!

He looks lost and afraid.

The tall buildings scare him.

And he's never seen so many people.

"Don't worry," I tell him.
"The buildings won't hurt you,
and most of the people are friendly."

"How did you get here?" I ask.

"I climbed in to have a nap," he explains,

"and when I woke up, I was *lost!*"

"I'll help you. Tell me where you live."

"There are trees where I live," he tells me.

So we find some trees.

"More trees," he says, "and water!"

I take him to a place where there are more
trees — and water, too.
"No," he says. "This is not it either."

I have an idea.

"Follow me!" I say.

I take him to a tall building.

We go inside, get on the elevator,
and ride all the way to the top.

From up here we can see the whole city.
"Look!" I say. "Now we can find your home."
"There it is!" he says, pointing.

Down we go, across three streets
and into the park.

The park is not the bear's home after all —
but he likes it there.
We go for a boat ride,

we have lunch,

and we go to the playground.

We are having a good time.
But it is getting late, and the bear is still lost.

"Let's try the library," I tell him.
"We can find out anything here!"
Inside the library we look through lots of books.

The bear sees a picture that looks like his home. We find the place on a map and hurry outside.

A bus is leaving.

We get on the bus and ride for a long time.

Finally, we are there.

"*This* is where I live!" says the bear.

He gives me a hug and thanks me again for my help.

Then he waves good-bye and disappears into the forest.

The trees are so tall, and there aren't any people.
"Wait!" I call to the bear, "come back!"
"I think I'm lost!" I tell him.

"Don't worry," he says.
"I will help you."

Lost!

David McPhail

Think About the Story

1. How else could the boy have helped the bear?

2. Do you think the boy found his way home? Why?

3. What would you do if you got lost?

Go on a Web Field Trip

Visit Education Place and explore the city where the bear got lost.

www.eduplace.com/kids

City and Country Mural

Compare the boy's home in the city with the bear's home in the country. Then make a group mural. Draw and label things for each place.

Taxi   Forest

Expressing

Write a Journal Entry

How would it feel to be lost? Write some sentences about it in your journal.

Tips
- **List your ideas in a word web.**
- **Use describing words.**

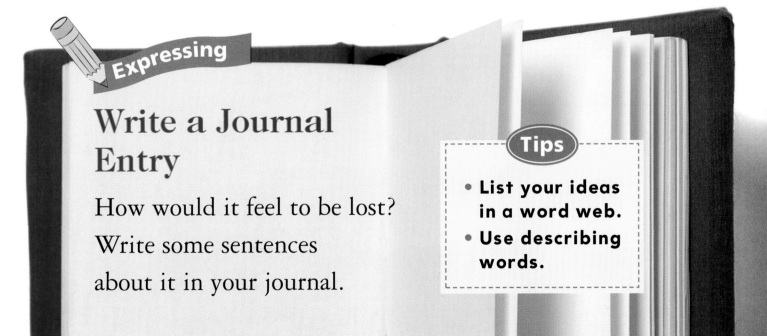

Skill: How to Read a Diagram

- **Read** the title of the diagram.

- **Look** at the labels. They name the parts.

- **Think** about what each part does.

On the Move

by Henry Pluckrose

Machines help people travel quickly and carry heavy loads.

The **space shuttle** is a machine. It carries astronauts into space.

Bicycle

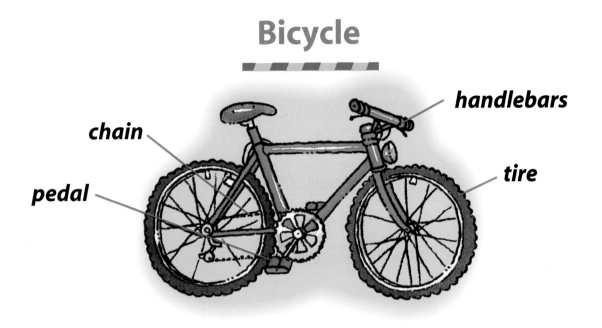

chain

pedal

handlebars

tire

A **bicycle** is a machine.
The faster you pedal,
the faster you move.

73

Airplanes are machines that fly. A jumbo jet can carry more than 300 passengers.

Trains run on specially built railway tracks.

Airplane

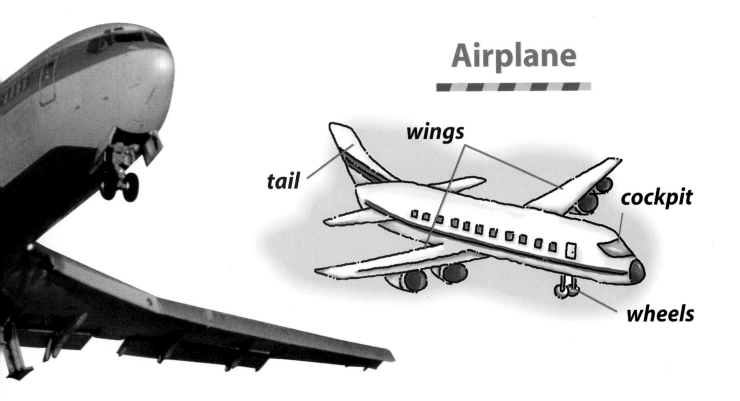

tail

wings

cockpit

wheels

Signs Ahead!

Look at the signs. Where might you see them? What do the signs tell you?

STOP

RAILROAD CROSSING 2 TRACKS

BIKE ROUTE

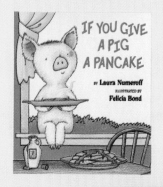

Build a House

What happens when a pig gets a pancake? Read the next story to find out.

Words to Know

old	build
piece	you
shoes	too
start	through
under	glue
very	might
wear	

Practice Sentences

1. You can build a house.
2. Wear old clothes and old shoes.
3. Set some wood under a tree.
4. Start with one piece of wood and some glue.
5. You might paint the house, too.
6. The house will look very good when you're through!

Meet the Author

Laura Numeroff read six books every week when she was growing up! Now her favorite job is writing children's books.

Meet the Illustrator

Felicia Bond decided to become an artist when she was five years old. Her first job was drawing a class mural when she was only six. Now she draws pictures for books.

Internet

Read more about Laura Numeroff and Felicia Bond at Education Place.
www.eduplace.com/kids

78

IF YOU GIVE
A PIG
A PANCAKE

BY **Laura Numeroff**

ILLUSTRATED BY
Felicia Bond

Strategy Focus

Read Together   As you read, ask yourself if
the story events could really happen.

If you give a pig a pancake,

she'll want some syrup to go with it.

You'll give her some of your favorite
maple syrup. She'll probably get all sticky,
so she'll want to take a bath.

She'll ask you for
some bubbles.

When you give her the bubbles,
she'll probably ask you for a toy.
You'll have to find your rubber duck.

The duck will remind her of the farm where she was born.
She might feel homesick and want to visit her family.

She'll want you to come too.
She'll look through your closet
for a suitcase.

Then she'll look under your bed.

When she's under the bed,
she'll find your old tap shoes.

She'll try them on. She'll probably
need something special to
wear with them.

89

When she's all dressed, she'll ask for some music.

You'll play your
very best piano piece,
and she'll start dancing.

Then she'll want you to take her picture.

So you'll have to get your camera.

When she sees the picture,

she'll ask you to take more.

Then she'll want to send one to each of her friends.

You'll have to give her
some envelopes and stamps

and take her to the mailbox.

On the way, she'll see the tree in your backyard.
She'll want to build a tree house.

So you'll have to get her some wood,
a hammer, and some nails.

When the tree house is finished,
she'll want to decorate it.

She'll ask for wallpaper and glue.
When she hangs the wallpaper,
she'll get all sticky.

Feeling sticky will remind her
of your favorite maple syrup.
She'll probably ask you for some.

And chances are,
if she asks you for some syrup,

she'll want a pancake to go with it.

Think About the Story

1. What is the problem in the story?

2. What do you think the girl will do the next time a pig asks for a pancake?

3. Would you give the pig a pancake? Why?

Internet

Take an Online Poll

What was the funniest thing the pig did in the story? Visit Education Place and vote!

www.eduplace.com/kids

Designing a Tree House

1. Make a list of the things you would need to build a tree house.

2. Draw a picture of your tree house and label the parts.

3. Share your work with the group.

Narrating

Write a Story

Write about three more things that might happen after the pig gets a pancake.

Tips

- Use a capital letter at the beginning of each sentence.
- End each sentence with a period.

Blueberry Pancakes

Ingredients

Dry Mix

Sift together:

3/4 cup flour

1/2 teaspoon salt

1 tablespoon sugar

1 teaspoon baking powder

1 egg

3/4 cup milk

1 tablespoon melted butter

1/2 cup blueberries

syrup

Directions

1. Crack the egg into a bowl.
2. Stir in the milk and the melted butter.
3. Stir the dry mix into the bowl.
4. Heat some extra butter in a pan.
5. Drop 1/2 cup of the batter into the pan.
6. Flip the pancake and cook it.
7. Drop 7 blueberries on top. Add syrup and eat!

The Food Groups

Eat foods from each group every day.
Try not to eat too many fats and sweets.

·············· Grains ·····················

············· Fruits ·············

············· Dairy ·············

Vegetables

Meats

Fats and Sweets

Read Together

✔ Writing a Personal Response

Some tests ask you to read a question and write an answer that tells what you think. Here is a sample.

- **Read the directions carefully so you know what to do.**

- **Look for key words that tell you what to write about.**

- **Think about what you will write.**

- **After you finish writing, read your sentences and correct any mistakes.**

In the theme *We Can Work It Out*, the children find ways to fix problems. Have you ever had to solve a problem? Write some sentences about what you did to solve the problem.

Now look at a good answer a student wrote.

I lost my library book. I was sad. I asked my friend Ellen to help me find it. We looked on the playground. We looked in Ms. Wood's room, too. Then I found the book in my red backpack.

The sentences tell about the question.

The sentences tell what the writer thinks.

The sentences include interesting details.

Plays

What is a play?

- A play is a story told mainly through the words of the characters. It can be read aloud or acted out.

- Sometimes a play has a narrator, who tells what is happening in the play.

- Each character's name appears before the words he or she speaks.

- When you take part in a play, read the character's words the way you think the character might say them.

Contents

The Lion and the Mouse

Characters:	Narrator
	Mouse
	Lion

Narrator: Once upon a time, a little mouse lived in the jungle.

Mouse: I love to run and play under the light of the moon.

Narrator: One night the mouse left his den.

Lion: ROAR!

Narrator: A big lion with big teeth was waiting right outside!

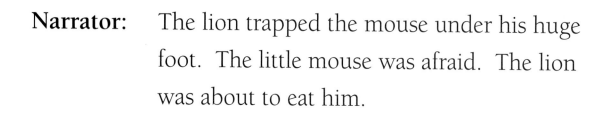

Narrator: The lion trapped the mouse under his huge foot. The little mouse was afraid. The lion was about to eat him.

Mouse: Please, Mr. Lion, let me go.

Lion: Why should I let you go?

Mouse: You are the King of the Jungle and I
             am too small to make a meal for you.
             And if you let me go, someday I will
             help you.

Narrator: The lion shook his head, but he let the mouse go.

Mouse: Thank you very much, Mr. Lion. If you ever need me, just call.

Lion: Ha, ha, ha! How could a big lion ever need a little mouse like you? Go run and play.

Narrator: The mouse ran away. But he had not gone very far when there was a big roar.

Mouse: Mr. Lion might be hurt. I'll just go back and check.

Narrator: The mouse found the lion trapped in a big net. Each time the lion tried to get out, he got more stuck in the net. Now the lion was trapped for good.

Mouse: Don't be afraid, Mr. Lion. I can help you.

Lion: You? You are too small. Run away before the hunters come.

Mouse: Just give me a chance. You'll see what I can do.

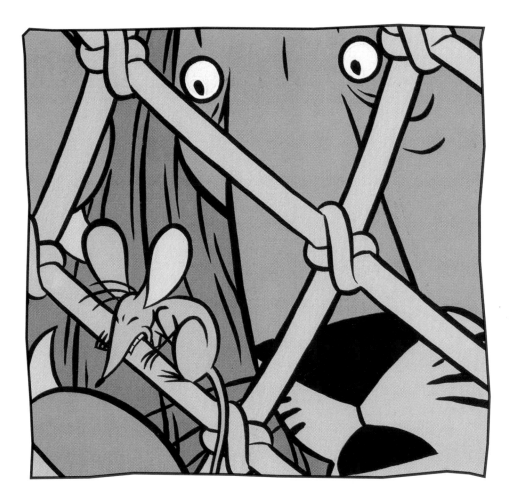

Narrator: The mouse started to chew on the net. At last, one rope broke. Then another rope broke. The mouse was tired, but he knew he couldn't stop. He had to save the lion.

Narrator: At last, there was a big hole in the net.

Mouse: Run, Mr. Lion! Get out of the net fast. I hear the hunters!

Lion: I'm trying, but I can't fit through this hole.

Narrator: The lion pushed and pushed to get out of the net. With one last jump, he landed outside the net.

Narrator: The lion was glad.

Lion: Thank you, little mouse. Without you, the hunters would have trapped me. I didn't think one as small as you could do much, but you have been a big help.

Mouse: If you hadn't let me go, Mr. Lion, I couldn't have helped you.

Narrator: That night, the two friends went out to run and play under the light of the moon.

Write a Play

You can write your own play. Here's how:

1. Think of a story you want to tell or retell.

2. Decide where your play takes place.

3. Choose the characters. Decide if there will be a narrator.

4. Write each character's name and what you want that character to say.

When you are finished, share your play with others. You might even act out your play!

128

Other Plays to Read

Easy-to-Read Folk and Fairy Tale Plays

by Carol Pugliano (Scholastic)

Six plays include *The Little Red Hen* and *The Bremen Town Musicians*.

25 Emergent Reader Plays Around the Year

by Carol Pugliano-Martin (Scholastic)

Short plays for all year long.

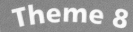

OUR EARTH

Read Together

Enjoy the Earth

Enjoy the earth gently
Enjoy the earth gently
For if the earth is spoiled
It cannot be repaired
Enjoy the earth gently

a Yoruba poem from Africa

131

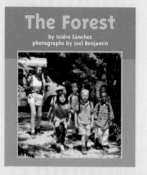

The Forest
by Isidro Sánchez
photographs by Joel Benjamin

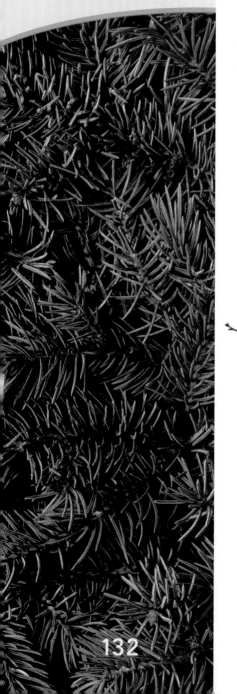

A Trip to the Forest

In the next story you read, you will find out about a class field trip to the forest.

Words to Know

about	tiny
because	tells
draw	loves
happy	planted
teacher	added
part	

Practice Sentences

1. We ask our teacher about her day in the forest.

2. She tells us how she planted a tiny tree.

3. She has added to part of the forest.

4. We draw a picture of the forest.

5. Our teacher is happy because she loves the picture!

Meet the Author and the Photographer

Besides this book, **Isidro Sánchez** has written books about skiing and mountain climbing in both Spanish and English. He likes to show children how much fun nature can be!

Joel Benjamin has been taking pictures for over twenty years. His advice for getting a great smile in a picture is to have the person say "snake" instead of "cheese!"

Internet

You can find out more about Isidro Sánchez and Joel Benjamin at Education Place.

www.eduplace.com/kids

The Forest

by Isidro Sánchez
photographs by Joel Benjamin

Read Together When you finish reading, use your own words to tell what you learned about the forest.

Today our class is taking a trip to the forest! We will learn about the plants and trees that grow there. We will also learn about the animals that make their home in the forest.

Our teacher tells us, "This is a pine tree. The squirrel loves the tiny nuts that grow inside the pinecones."

"This tall tree is a spruce. It has pinecones that hang down."

 "This big oak tree has a very thick trunk.
Squirrels eat its acorns."

"You can tell what tree a leaf is from by its color and shape. It is fun to look at leaves."

"The trees in the forest give us wood for paper and homes, and many other things we need."

142

"We must be very careful in the forest. One spark can start a big forest fire. The fires kill the trees and hurt the animals."

143

We like the forest. It is very beautiful and is home for many interesting birds, bugs, animals, and plants.

Many different types of mushrooms also grow in the forest. But we must be careful not to take any, because they may be poisonous!

We sit in the forest and draw pictures of trees. Then we label every part of the tree — the leaves, branches, trunk, and bark.

We dig holes and plant little trees ourselves.
We tie them to stakes to keep them straight,
press the soil down, and water them well.

When they grow, we will be proud to have planted these trees and happy that we have added something to the beautiful forest!

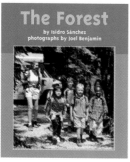

The Forest
by Isidro Sánchez
photographs by Joel Benjamin

Think About the Story

1. What do you think was the best part of the trip to the forest? Why?

2. Why do you think the children planted trees at the end of the story?

3. Why is it important to have forests?

Internet

Go on a Web Field Trip

Visit Education Place to explore a forest.

www.eduplace.com/kids

It Comes from Trees

Look around. What do you see that's made from wood? Make a list of things that can be made from trees. Share your list with the group.

paper
houses
tables

Explaining

Write a Forest Guide

Fold some sheets of paper in half to make a book. On each page, draw something from the forest, label it, and write a sentence to tell about it.

Tips
- **Use what you learned from the story.**
- **Write a fact about each picture.**

Acorn

Skill: How to Read a Pamphlet

- **Read** the title.

- **See** how you can use the information.

- **Think** about why the pamphlet was written.

Saving the Earth

152

 Don't litter.
Animals and birds can get hurt from eating litter.

 Hang a bird feeder outside.
You'll be helping birds get food through the cold winter.

3 Instead of riding in a car, try riding a bike, walking, or going on a bus. Using less gas will help keep the air clean.

4 Turn out the lights when you don't need them. Using less electricity will help keep the air and water clean.

5 Turn off the water when you brush your teeth. You'll save at least five gallons of water.

6 Recycle glass, plastic, metal, and paper. Some of these things can be used again to make something new.

A Research Report

A research report tells facts about a topic in the writer's own words. Use this student's writing as a model when you write a research report of your own.

A research report tells **facts** about the topic.

Ladybug

My report is about the ladybug. This insect has six legs, two wings, and no antennae. It lives in gardens. This insect likes to eat other insects that are harmful to plants.

Something interesting about this insect is that it is carnivorous. This means it eats meat, not plants. It can also be called the ladybird beetle. It is helpful to people because it destroys garden pests. This insect is about the same size as a finger is wide.

Tori S.
Grade: one
State: Florida
Hobbies: reading and swimming
What she'd like to be when she grows up: a first-grade teacher

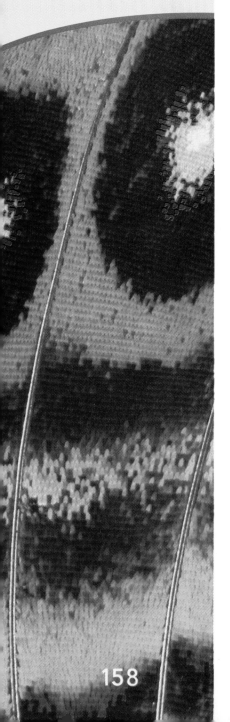

What Could It Be?

Do you want to see a caterpillar change into a butterfly? Then read the next story.

Words to Know

always	now
eight	how
arms	flowers
seven	pouch
warm	out
ready	about
body	
yellow	

Practice Sentences

1. Here's a small yellow egg.
2. Look what's come out of the egg!
3. Look at its body and its arms and legs.
4. Now what could it be?
5. The animal is ready to leave its warm pouch.
6. In about seven or eight weeks it can fly to flowers.
7. It's always hungry.
8. How about that? It's a butterfly!

Meet the Author and the Photographer

Mary Ling has written more than ten books on how animals grow and live in nature. Her books teach children interesting facts about animals. She has written about jets and dump trucks, too!

Kim Taylor likes nature and science. He has taken pictures for books about fossils, rain, and nighttime animals.

Internet

To find out more about Mary Ling and Kim Taylor, visit Education Place.

www.eduplace.com/kids

160

SEE HOW THEY GROW

BUTTERFLY

Read Together   As you read, think about whether the author does a good job of providing information on butterflies.

161

Out of the egg

 I am a caterpillar. I grow inside my tiny yellow egg, which is about the size of this dot __.

My mother is a butterfly. One day I will look like her.

I am ready to hatch, so I chew a hole in my eggshell.

I squeeze out of the hole.

At last I am free!

Growing bigger

I am one week old.
Each day I grow in size.
I am always hungry.

My skin feels very
tight. I am starting
to shed my skin.

I squeeze out of my old skin.
My new skin fits my plump body.

Soon I grow too big for this skin.

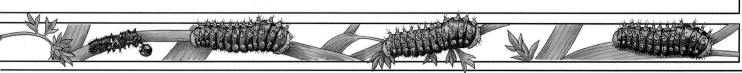

Lots of legs

I am two weeks old and
my skin is splitting again.

Now I have bright stripes on my body.

How many arms and legs do I have? I have six arms and ten legs.

Striped suits

I am three weeks old.
I am munching a
good plant.

Other caterpillars
are eating it, too.
I go on to the next
plant.

While I am eating, my striped suit hides me from danger.

I use my orange horn to scare enemies away.

Changing shape

I am four weeks old. Now I am a
full-grown caterpillar.

I look for a safe
hiding place.

My body is
changing shape.

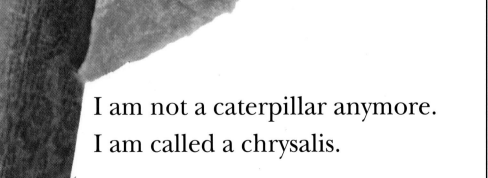

I am not a caterpillar anymore.
I am called a chrysalis.

Wings at last

When I am seven weeks old,
I climb out of my pouch.
I am a butterfly.

My new wings are
folded and wet.

I rest for a while in
the warm sunshine.

Soon my wings are flat.
I can fly!

In the sunshine

Now I am eight
weeks old and fully
grown. My wings
are strong. I can fly
here and there.

I use my long tongue to drink sweet nectar from the flowers.

At last I look like my mother!

See how I grew

The egg

One week old

Two weeks old

Three weeks old

Four weeks old

Seven weeks old

Eight weeks old

Think About the Story

1. How is the butterfly like the caterpillar? How is it different?

2. Why does the caterpillar shed its skin?

3. Would you like to watch a caterpillar turn into a butterfly? Why?

Internet

Build a Story

How does a caterpillar turn into a butterfly? Go to Education Place to put the stages in the right order.

www.eduplace.com/kids

Matching Parts

Cut out half a butterfly shape from a
folded sheet of paper. Unfold the paper.
Look at how the two halves are the exact
same shape. Now decorate your butterfly!

1.   **2.**   **3.**

Describing

Write a Description

Write some sentences to describe
the caterpillar or the butterfly.

Tips

- Use words that will help
  a reader get a picture in
  his or her mind.
- Check your spelling.

Read
Together

Skill: How to Look at Fine Art

- **Look** at the picture. How does it make you feel?

- **Think** about what the artist is trying to show you.

R.Mervilus

Landscape with Trees and Animals, R. Mervilus, Haitian

EARTH

E is for Earth

A is for Animals

R is for Respect

T is for Trees

H is for Home — what the Earth is.

by Star, Age 9
Lac La Ronge Band Treaty Cree,
Saskatchewan, Canada

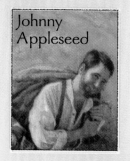

On the Move

Find out why a man was called Johnny Appleseed when you read the next story.

Words to Know

carry	work
kind	person
put	liked
saw	stopped
butter	moving
were	

Practice Sentences

1. John and Jack were moving to a new house.
2. Each person had to carry something and put it in the van.
3. It was hard work.
4. Soon John saw that it was noon.
5. So John and Jack stopped to eat lunch.
6. They both liked the same kind of lunch — bread and butter.

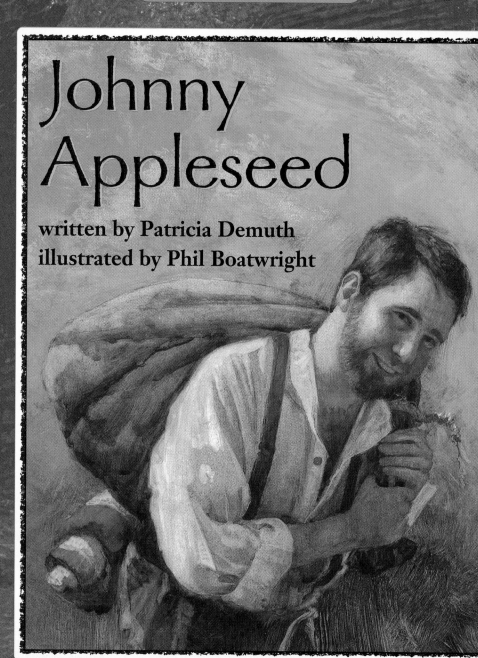

Johnny Appleseed

written by Patricia Demuth

illustrated by Phil Boatwright

Strategy Focus

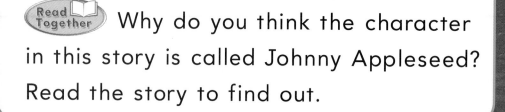

Read Together   Why do you think the character in this story is called Johnny Appleseed? Read the story to find out.

184

Who was Johnny Appleseed?
Was he just in stories?
No. Johnny was a real person.

His name was John Chapman. He planted apple trees — lots and lots of them. So people called him Johnny Appleseed.

Johnny was young when our country was young. Back then many people were moving West.

There were no towns, no schools, and not many houses. And there were no apple trees.

Johnny was going West, too. He wanted
to plant apple trees. He wanted to make
the West a nicer place to live.

So Johnny got a big, big bag. He filled
it with apple seeds. Then he set out.

Johnny walked for days and weeks. On and on. Soon his clothes were rags. He had no shoes.

And what kind of hat did he wear? A cooking pot! That way he didn't have to carry it.

191

Snow came.

Did Johnny stop?

No.

He made snowshoes.

Then he walked some more.

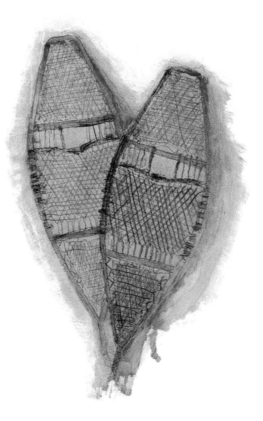

Spring came. Johnny was out West now. He stopped by a river. He dug a hole. Inside he put an apple seed. Then he put dirt over the seed.

Someday an apple tree would stand here. Johnny set out again. He had lots more seeds to plant.

Johnny walked by himself. But he was not alone. The animals were his friends.

Most people were afraid of animals. But not Johnny.

One day a big, black bear saw Johnny go by. It did not hurt Johnny. Maybe the bear knew Johnny was a friend.

The Indians were Johnny's friends, too.
They showed him how to find good
food — plants and roots.

Where did Johnny sleep?
Under the stars. Johnny liked to lie
on his back and look up. The wind
blew. Owls hooted. The stars winked
down at him.

Many years passed. Johnny planted apple
trees everywhere. People started to call
him Johnny Appleseed.

One day he came back to where he had planted the first seed. It was a big tree now. A girl was swinging in it.

That night Johnny stayed with the girl's family. He told stories. Everybody liked Johnny.

"Stay with us," they said. "Make a home here."

But Johnny did not stay.
"I have work to do," he said. "I am happy. The whole world is my home."

More and more people came out West.
Johnny planted more and more trees. In
the spring, the trees bloomed with white
flowers.

In the fall, there were apples — red,
round, ripe apples.

People made apple pies. And apple butter for their bread. And apple cider to drink. And children had apple trees to climb.

It was all thanks to Johnny Appleseed.

Meet the Author and the Illustrator

Johnny Appleseed
written by Patricia Demuth
illustrated by Phil Boatwright

As a child, **Patricia Demuth** spent her time singing, bike riding, and reading on her family's sheep farm. She hopes children will care more about the Earth after reading her books.

Phil Boatwright likes to use people he knows as models for the characters he paints. When he's not painting, Phil Boatwright likes to plant seeds in his own garden.

Internet

To find out more about Patricia Demuth and Phil Boatwright, visit Education Place.

www.eduplace.com/kids

207

Read Together

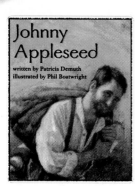

Johnny
Appleseed
written by Patricia Demuth
illustrated by Phil Boatwright

Think About the Story

1. Do you think Johnny Appleseed helped to make the world a better place? Why?

2. Why do people remember Johnny Appleseed today?

3. Would you like to have met Johnny Appleseed? Why?

Internet

Send an E-postcard

Send an e-postcard to tell a friend about *Johnny Appleseed.* You can find a postcard at Education Place.

www.eduplace.com/kids

Talk About Johnny Appleseed

Work with a partner. Take turns telling what happened in Johnny Appleseed's life from beginning to end.

Tips

- **Listen to your partner.**
- **Wait until your partner has finished before you start talking.**

Reflecting

Write a Journal Entry

What could you do today to change the world in the future? Write about it in your journal.

Tip

- **Think about what you want to say before you write.**

recycle

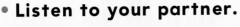

Skill: How to Read a Time Line

- **Read** the time line from left to right.

- **Read** the words on the time line. They tell you when things happen.

Life Cycle of an Apple

by Angela Royston

An apple is a fruit that grows on a tree. Every year each tree gives a new crop of apples.

① Apple Tree, late winter

The trees have no leaves during the cold months of winter. Each twig has tight buds.

1. late winter ▶ ▶ ▶ ▶ ▶ ▶ ▶ ▶

Inside the bud are tiny leaves. They push through the bud and grow big.

③ one week later

Pink buds are growing in the leaves.

2. early spring ▶ ▶ ▶ ▶

3. one week later ▶ ▶ ▶ ▶

 Blossom and Pollination, spring

The pink buds turn into small pinkish-white flowers called blossoms. The flowers have a yellow dust called pollen.

This honeybee collects pollen and stores it on sticky hairs on its back legs. This pollen helps to make tiny apple seeds.

The petals shrink and fall off, leaving a tiny apple with the apple seeds inside. The apples start to swell and grow.

6 **Harvest, early fall**

All summer the apples grow big and sweet. These big red apples are now sweet and ripe and ready for picking.

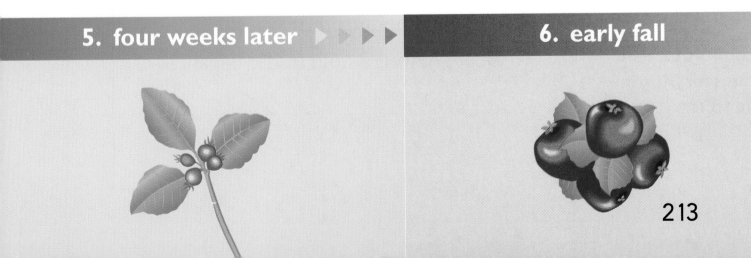

5. four weeks later ▶ ▶ ▶ ▶   **6. early fall**

Read Together

✔ Choosing the Best Answer

How do you choose the best answer on a test? Look at this sample test for *Butterfly*. The right answer is marked.

Tips

- Read the directions carefully.

- Read the question. Read all the answers.

- Fill in the whole circle.

- Look back at the story if you need to.

Read the question. Fill in the circle next to the best answer.

1 How did the caterpillar hatch from the egg?

○ It flew out of the eggshell.
○ It had help from its mother.
● It chewed a hole in the eggshell.

Now see how one student chose the right answer.

I am looking for the answer that tells how the caterpillar hatched. The first answer isn't right because caterpillars don't fly.

The second answer isn't right because the caterpillar didn't get help from its mother.

Now I see why the last answer is the right choice.

Glossary

A

acorns
An **acorn** is a nut that grows into an oak tree. Squirrels like to eat **acorns**.

agree
To **agree** means to share the same idea. John and Maria always **agree** about which movie to see.

apple
An **apple** is a kind of fruit. **Apples** can have red, yellow, or green skin.

B

beautiful
Beautiful means very nice to look at or hear. We saw a **beautiful** sunset at the beach.

book

A **book** is a group of pages with words and pictures. I went to the library to find a **book** about tigers.

born

Born means brought into life. The baby lamb was **born** in the barn.

branches

A **branch** is part of a tree. The leaves of the tree grow on **branches**.

bread

Bread is a kind of food. You can make sandwiches with two pieces of **bread**.

bubbles

A **bubble** is a round ball of air. Jason likes to blow soap **bubbles**.

building

A **building** is a place where people live or keep things. Houses, schools, and stores are all **buildings**.

butterfly

A **butterfly** is an insect with wings. A caterpillar will change into a **butterfly**.

C

candy bars

A **candy bar** is a sweet kind of food that is long and flat. There are many **candy bars** for sale at the store.

careful

To be **careful** means to do something slowly to make sure nothing bad happens. Be **careful** when you cross the street.

caterpillar

A **caterpillar** is an insect that looks like a worm. The **caterpillar** became a beautiful butterfly.

changing

To **change** means to become different. My puppy keeps **changing** as it gets older.

chrysalis

A **chrysalis** is like a cocoon. A butterfly comes out of a **chrysalis**.

cider

Cider is a drink made from apples. You make **cider** by pressing the juice out of apples.

city

A **city** is a place where many people live and work. There are many tall buildings in the **city** where I live.

closet

A **closet** is a very small room. I put my coat in the **closet**.

clothes

Clothes are things you wear. Shirts and pants are kinds of **clothes**.

crayons

A **crayon** is a piece of colored wax used for drawing and writing. Pat used her **crayons** to draw a picture of a zoo.

D

danger
Danger is something that can hurt you. Big storms can put people in **danger**.

different
Different means not the same. Red and blue are **different** colors.

disappears
To **disappear** means to stop being seen. Sometimes the sun **disappears** behind the clouds.

E

elevator
An **elevator** is a small room that takes you up and down in a building. The **elevator** took us to the top floor.

enemies
An **enemy** is a person or animal that wants to hurt another. Cats are the **enemies** of mice.

F

fault
If something is your **fault**, you are to blame.
It was my **fault** that the book got wet because
I left it outside.

favorite
Favorite means what you like the most. Luke's
favorite color is red.

food
Food is what people or animals eat.
People need **food** to live.

friendly
To be **friendly** means to like to meet people.
A **friendly** dog wags its tail when it meets
a person.

H

hoptoad
Hoptoad is another name for toad. A
hoptoad looks something like a frog.

I

interesting

Interesting means holding your attention.
The book was so **interesting** that Max couldn't
stop reading.

L

lemonade

Lemonade is a drink made from lemon
juice, water, and sugar. Larry drinks
lemonade on hot summer days.

library

A **library** is a place where many books are
kept. People can borrow books from a **library**.

M

maple syrup

Maple syrup is a sweet liquid made from the
sap of maple trees. Jen put **maple syrup** on
her pancakes.

music
Music is pleasing sounds made by instruments or voices. The band played **music**.

N

nectar
Nectar is a sweet liquid found in flowers.
Bees gather **nectar** to make honey.

O

orange
Orange is a color. A pumpkin is **orange**.

P

park
A **park** is a place where people go to enjoy being outside. The city **park** has lots of grass and trees.

piano

A **piano** is a kind of musical instrument. A **piano** has many black and white keys.

poisonous

A **poison** is something that can cause sickness or death. A rattlesnake has a **poisonous** bite.

probably

Probably means that you are almost sure something is true. I will **probably** stay at home today because I don't feel well.

R

remind

To **remind** means to help someone remember something. **Remind** me to return the book so I won't forget.

river

A **river** is a wide path of water that has land on both sides. The water in this **river** moves very fast.

S

scare

To **scare** means to make afraid. The barking dog will **scare** the cat.

share

To **share** means to let everyone have some. It's always nice to **share** something with a friend.

stories

A **story** is a group of words that tell what happened to people and places. I like to read **stories** about sports.

suit

A **suit** is a set of clothes that match. The caterpillar looks like it is wearing a striped **suit**.

T

toys

A **toy** is something to play with. My favorite **toys** are trucks and balls.

types
A **type** is a group of things that have something in common. There are many **types** of flowers.

W

worry
To **worry** means to feel that something bad might happen. I **worry** when my hamster gets out of its cage.

Y

years
A **year** is 365 days. My little sister will go to school in two **years**.

young
To be **young** means to have been alive only a short time. **Young** is the opposite of old.

Acknowledgments

For each of the selections listed below, grateful acknowledgment is made for permission to excerpt and/or reprint original or copyrighted material, as follows:

Selections

Butterfly, by Mary Ling, photographs by Kim Taylor. Copyright © 1992 by Dorling Kindersley Limited, London. Reprinted by permission of Dorling Kindersley Publishing, Inc.

The Forest, by I. Sánchez and C. Peris. Copyright © 1991 by Barron's Educational Series, Inc. Reprinted by permission of Barron's Educational Series, Inc.

If You Give a Pig a Pancake, by Laura Numeroff, illustrated by Felicia Bond. Text copyright © 1998 by Laura Numeroff. Illustrations copyright © 1998 by Felicia Bond. Reprinted by permission of HarperCollins Publishers.

Johnny Appleseed, by Patricia Demuth. Text copyright © 1996 by Patricia Demuth. Reprinted by permission of Grosset & Dunlap Inc, a division of Penguin Putnam Inc.

Selection from Life Cycle of an Apple, by Angela Royston. Copyright © 1998 by Angela Royston. Reprinted by permission of Reed Educational & Professional Publishing, a division of Heinemann Publishers, Oxford.

Illustrations from *The Lion and the Mouse,* originally published as *El León y el Ratón,* by Max. Illustrations copyright © 1993 by Max. Reprinted by permission of La Galera, S.A.

Lost!, by David McPhail. Copyright © 1990 by David McPhail. Reprinted by permission of Little, Brown and Company (Inc.).

On the Move, by Henry Pluckrose. Copyright © 1998 by Franklin Watts. Reprinted by permission of Franklin Watts, a division of Grolier Publishing.

That Toad Is Mine!, by Barbara Shook Hazen, illustrated by Jane Manning. Text copyright © 1998 by Barbara Shook Hazen. Illustrations copyright © 1998 by Jane Manning. Reprinted by permission of HarperCollins Publishers.

Poetry

"Earth" by Star, Cree, age 9 from *Women of the Native Struggle,* by Ronnie Farley, Orion Publishing 1993. Copyright © 1993 by Star Trudell. Reprinted by permission of John Trudell.

"Enjoy the Earth" originally titled *"Yoruba Poem"* as it appeared in *Earthways, Earthwise: Poems on Conservation,* selected by Judith Nicholls. Published by Oxford University Press Children's Books, 1993.

"Hug O' War" from *Where the Sidewalk Ends,* by Shel Silverstein. Copyright © 1974 by Evil Eye Music, Inc. Reprinted by permission of HarperCollins Publishers.

"Sharing" from *Falling Up,* by Shel Silverstein. Copyright © 1996 by Shel Silverstein. Reprinted by permission of HarperCollins Publishers.

"When My Friends All Moved Away," by Steven Kroll. Copyright © 1977 by Steven Kroll. Reprinted by permission of the author.

Special thanks to the following teachers whose students' compositions appear as Student Writing Models: Cheryl Claxton, Florida; Patricia Kopay, Delaware; Susana Llanes, Michigan; Joan Rubens, Delaware; Nancy Schulten, Kentucky; Linda Wallis, California

Credits

Photography

3 (t) StockByte. **8** images Copyright © 2000 PhotoDisc, Inc. **12** (icon) StockByte. (bkgd) image Copyright © 2000 PhotoDisc, Inc. **14** (l) image Copyright © 2000 PhotoDisc, Inc. **16** (t) Tom Ianuzzi/Mercury Pictures. **17** (bkgd) image Copyright © 2000 PhotoDisc, Inc. **42** AP Photo/Gary Dineen. **45** (l) Stephen Krasemann/Tony Stone Images. (r) Johnny Johnson/Tony Stone Images. **46** Sharron McElmeel. **72** Sipa Press. **73** Rubberball

Productions. **74** (b) QA Photos Ltd. **74–5** (t) Scott Barrow/International Stock. **75** (bl) Comstock KLIPS. (bm) (br) images Copyright © 2000 PhotoDisc, Inc. **78** (t) Micheal Justice/Mercury Pictures. (b) Andrew Yates/Mercury Pictures. **108** (tl) (tr) (middle row) (bottom row) Artville. (tm) Corbis Royalty Free. **109** (tl) (trm) (tr) (ml) (mlm) (mr) (bm) (br) Artville. (tlm) (mrm) Image Ideas. (bl) Comstock KLIPS. **128** Nancy Sheehan/PhotoEdit. **130** (icon) image Copyright © 2000 PhotoDisc, Inc. (bkgd) DigitalVision. **130–1** Jim Cummins/FPG International. **132** (t) David Young-Wolff/Tony Stone Images. (b) images Copyright © 2000 PhotoDisc, Inc. **134** (b) Mark Gardner. (frame) Image Farm. **135** (bkgd) image Copyright © 2000 PhotoDisc, Inc. **137** (t) David Young-Wolff/Tony Stone Images. **138** (b) image Copyright © 2000 PhotoDisc, Inc. **139** (b) image Copyright © 2000 PhotoDisc, Inc. **140** (b) image Copyright © 2000 PhotoDisc, Inc. **141** (b) image Copyright © 2000 PhotoDisc, Inc. **142** images Copyright © 2000 PhotoDisc, Inc. **143** Tony Stone Images. **144** (b) Corbis Royalty Free. **145** (b) Artville. **149** (r) image Copyright © 2000 PhotoDisc, Inc. **153** image Copyright © 2000 PhotoDisc, Inc. **154** (t) Rubberball Productions. **155** (t) image Copyright © 2000 PhotoDisc, Inc. (b) © Myrleen Cate/Photo Network/PictureQuest. **158** (l) Artville. **160** (t) StockByte. (b) image Copyright © 2000 PhotoDisc, Inc. **161** (bkgd) Artville. **180–1** Edmond Van Hoorick/SuperStock. **182** (l) Image Farm. **184** (bkgd) Image Farm. **207** Courtesy Phil Boatwright. **210** F. Merlet/A-Z Botanical Collection. **211** (t) F. Merlet/A-Z Botanical Collection. (b) Roger Scruton. **212** (t) Roger Scruton. (b) Holt Studios International/Nigel Cattlin. **213** (t) Roger Scruton. (b) Holt Studios International/Inga Spence. **216** (t) image Copyright © 2000 PhotoDisc, Inc. (b) Artville. **218** (t) PhotoSpin. (b) Artville. **219** (t) Kim Taylor/Dorling Kindersley. **220** image Copyright © 2000 PhotoDisc, Inc. **221** (t) Artville. (b) image Copyright © 2000 PhotoDisc, Inc. **222** image Copyright © 2000 PhotoDisc, Inc. **223** John Elk/Tony Stone Images. **224** (t) Image Club. (b) © Frans Lanting/Minden Pictures. **225** Rubberball Productions. **226** image Copyright © 2000 PhotoDisc, Inc.

Assignment Photography
5 (top center, middle right) Joel Benjamin. **12, 13, 16** (b), **71, 105** (b), **106–7, 135–7, 140–1, 144–9, 152, 209** Joel Benjamin. **134** (b), **138–9** Mark Gardner. **39** Allan Landau. **111, 215** Tony Scarpetta.

Illustration
14–15 Melissa Iwai. **40, 41** Shel Silverstein. **70** Sally Vitsky. **73, 75** Teri Gower. **77** Nathan Jarvis. **133** Eleanor Adam. **150** Erin Terry. **159** Suling Wang. **183** Franklin Hammond. **184–208** Phil Boatwright.

228